PATTERNS OF PERCEPTION

Scholarly Articles by Peter Fritz Walter

PATTERNS
OF PERCEPTION

Preferred Pathways
to Genius

by Peter Fritz Walter

Published by Sirius-C Media Galaxy LLC

113 Barksdale Professional Center, Newark, Delaware, USA

Set in Avenir Light and Trajan Pro

Designed by Peter Fritz Walter

ISBN 978-1-517349-79-0

Publishing Categories
Psychology / Neuropsychology

Publisher Contact Information
publisher@sirius-c-publishing.com
http://sirius-c-publishing.com

Author Contact Information
pfw@peterfritzwalter.com

About Dr. Peter Fritz Walter
http://peterfritzwalter.com

About the Author

Parallel to an international law career in Germany, Switzerland and the United States, Dr. Peter Fritz Walter (Pierre) focused upon fine art, cookery, astrology, musical performance, social sciences and humanities.

He started writing essays as an adolescent and received a high school award for creative writing and editorial work for the school magazine.

After finalizing his law diplomas, he graduated with an LL.M. in European Integration at Saarland University, Germany, and with a Doctor of Law title from University of Geneva, Switzerland, in 1987.

He then took courses in psychology at the University of Geneva and interviewed a number of psychotherapists in Lausanne and Geneva, Switzerland. His interest was intensified through a hypnotherapy with an Ericksonian American hypnotherapist in Lausanne. This led him to the recovery and healing of his inner child.

In 1986, he met the late French psychotherapist and child psychoanalyst Françoise Dolto (1908-1988) in Paris and interviewed her. A long correspondence followed up to their encounter which was considered by the curators of the Dolto Trust interesting enough to be published in a book alongside all of Dolto's other letter exchanges by Gallimard Publishers in Paris, in 2005.

After a second career as a corporate trainer and personal coach, Pierre retired as a full-time writer, philosopher and consultant.

His nonfiction books emphasize a systemic, holistic, cross-cultural and interdisciplinary perspective, while his fiction works and short stories focus upon education, philosophy, perennial wisdom, and the poetic formulation of an integrative worldview.

Pierre is a German-French bilingual native speaker and writes English as his 4th language after German, Latin and French. He also reads source literature for his research works in Spanish, Italian, Portuguese, and Dutch. In addition, Pierre has notions of Thai, Khmer, Chinese and Japanese.

All of Pierre's books are hand-crafted and self-published, designed by the author. Pierre publishes via his Delaware company, Sirius-C Media Galaxy LLC, and under the imprints of IPUBLICA and SCM (Sirius-C Media).

Pierre's Amazon Author Page

http://www.amazon.com/Peter-Fritz-Walter/e/B00M2QN4SU

Pierre's Blog

https://medium.com/@pierrefwalter

CONTENTS

SCIENCE AND PERCEPTION

Why Perception is a Primary Scientific Research Topic

This paper is about perception, a subject scarcely discussed in modern science. And yet it is a primary scientific topic. And at the same time, it is one of the foremost subjects of true spirituality, the spirituality that is truth-seeking, not the one that is dogmatic and salvational.

Traditionally, this kind of spirituality was rather bound to the East, especially India, while the Occident was rather addicted to the salvational, dogmatic and moralizing kind of religion. And these trends are still valid today.

The Vedas, while written in a poetic language, are scientific in nature and proceed scientifically. Hinduism has dealt extensively with perception, and the best information sources are to be found there.

And even such a modern and non-traditional spiritual teacher as Krishnamurti devoted a great part of his teaching to the modes of perception and the factors that influence and manipulate perception.

—See Peter Fritz Walter, A Psychological Revolution: A Critical Essay on Krishnamurti's Teaching and Philosophy (Great Minds Series, Vol. 1), 2014/2017.

Krishnamurti, despite the apparent revolutionary character of his teaching, is based on tradition. In fact, his teaching is a naturally logical continuation of the teaching of the Buddha. And Buddha's teaching, how can it be otherwise, of course dealt with perception!

In the West, the obvious absence of any scientific in-depth study of the holistic process of perception has various reasons, one of them being the general focus of modern science upon mere information processing.

It is self-evident that mechanistic science can only look at the causal effects between the information that is stored in the memory surface, and the impact this knowledge has on our mind. Only holistic science can go beyond that limitation and see all the non-causal factors involved in perception, and which is first of all the knowledge how the integration of new information in the memory surface works.

Holistic science is contrary to common belief not a mere Utopia or project for a future society. It is part of perennial philosophy and has existed before Aristotle destroyed it in the West, and Confucius in the East. This holistic science was part of the greatest culture on earth that ever existed: Minoan Culture. And this holistic science was based upon direct perception. What is direct perception?

Direct perception is our natural and most intelligent mode of perception. It is the way our brain receives and stores information.

New research has fully corroborated the teaching of the old sages who said that learning must be holistic and whole-brain in order to be truly effective.

There was a historical shift around two millennia ago that led to a trend away from direct perception and toward information processing, archiving or mere information reproduction.

We can only wonder when we hear scientists state that generally we use only between about five to eight percent of our brain or of our creativity resources. Why are we so terribly unproductive, so utterly ineffective in our creativity, in our performance, in our achievements, despite this whole process called civilization, despite the introduction of school systems more than five hundred years ago, despite the printing press, Gutenberg and all the rest of it? It seems that after all we have remained in a truly primitive state of evolution.

The answer is clear: because we have based this nonsensical patriarchal civilization upon *information processing* instead of founding it on the laws of direct perception.

A child does not need Gutenberg to learn his or her first language because this language is picked up in a process of direct perception, by chunks, by patterns, by passive awareness. And not by conscious information reception, by instilled tidbits of grammar, by incoherent single elements that the human brain cannot readily perceive as it perceives what is coded in holistic patterns. Direct perception is patterned perception.

The purpose of this study is both to identify the causes of this tremendous waste of opportunity, and show possibilities to take action here and now to begin changing this state of affairs on an individual human level.

Changing collective consciousness comes about through multiple and repeated individual changes of consciousness. Once a sufficient number of individuals have lifted their consciousness on a higher evolutionary level, there will be a major paradigm shift in the whole system that makes that group or collective consciousness will reproduce this shift on a collective or group level, a national or international level. This is how all true civilization comes about: through changes and transformations of consciousness that came about individually and that gradually became collective.

All begins in the cell and then expands to still bigger patterns. Nature is programmed in a system of patterns that are holistically related to each other and where the information of the whole is contained in every single cell of the pattern. The pattern structure is typical for the information the brain receives and stores. New information is added-on to existing information. Without such connections that in neurology are called *preferred pathways*, memory as we know it is not thinkable.

The better the brain can manage to associate new input with existing patterns of information, the better the information storage will be, and thus the higher will be the memorization result.

> —The preferred pathways theory was not invented by Herbert James Campbell but he has done an excellent summary of all the research in his book 'The Pleasure Areas,' published in 1973, where he additionally explains the importance of pleasure, and the dichotomy pleasure-violence in the brain.

Another insight about preferred pathways is that the information flow is dependent on the number of preferred pathways in the neuronet of the brain.

These neuronal connections are built during the very first years of life and later can only be changed and expanded under very high intellectual effort. Hence the importance of effective, intelligent and whole-brain learning in early childhood.

This insight naturally coincides with biographical genius research that evidently shows the fact that, first, all geniuses are very astute learners during their first years of life, and second, they are lucky enough to grow in the environment and emotional climate supportive for the growth of their genius.

Our brain processes all intake of information automatically, passively, without a need for us to set a decision about it. So we are all naturally high-speed and total learners. This fact is tremendously important for the understanding of the functioning of the brain. There is namely a positive side and a negative side about it.

Positively, the passively organizing perception of our brain insures that we continuously receive and store information; continuously means without interruption, at any time of the day and the night; also during sleep and even in deep coma all the information from the five senses is perceived and stored in the subconscious memory, or low self, that is always awake, always active.

—The correspondence to modern psychology and perception research in tribal cultures is to be found in the Huna teaching of the Kahunas of Hawaii. See Max Freedom Long, The Secret Science at Work: The Huna Method as a Way of Life (1995), p. 15.

So the apparently passive functioning of the brain is actually a dynamically active process. The important point about it is that the organizer of the information is inside and not outside of the system.

To make this more clear, let us take two groups of children. The first group is raised freely so that they can pick up any information freely from their environment and grow, from the information they get, into what they are destined for. The second group, however, is strictly regulated, protected and warded off from any unprocessed information.

Which group, would you think, will be more intelligent and more creative, the first or the second one?

Of course the first one. Simply because in their case the freely organizing and unhindered system of their perception and the free flow of information, combined with high input made that their brains were working on high gear whereas in the second group creative learning processes have for the most part been impeded, blocked or even mutilated.

In the first group the organizer of the information is inside, within the children in form of their higher intelligence and wisdom that directs them to receive all the information they need, shutting out all other information; in the second group it is the adults who raise these children, their parents and teachers for the most part. We can also put it that way: in the first group it is divine intelligence that cares for those children's evolution, in the second case however, it is limited and short-sighted human willfulness.

This simple example also shows which high impact the early environment has on the development of our intelligence and our later use of the potential we've got.

I believe we all have got high or genius potential but only very few of us were exposed to the right combination of environmental support and have, in addition, developed the necessary creative will for freeing themselves from the blindfolding trap of conditioning.

And we need both those factors working in a positive sense if we are to fully develop our talents and creational power.

I am sure that people like Leonardo da Vinci, Albert Einstein, Pablo Picasso or Svjatoslav Richter, were they scored for the use of their creative resources, would probably reach up to eighty or even more percent of usage, while for the common individual the four to eight percent might be realistic.

One of the greatest errors of mankind consists in the assumption that this state of affairs could not be changed and was programmed into nature. Darwinism has contributed to create a kind of gigantic madness by building a huge evolutionary theory on this fundamental error, which is one of the most destructive and absurd lies about the human nature that have ever been thought of; and the hero cult has built it into the belief system of millions forming part and parcel of the modern and postmodern industrial culture.

What is true is that every single human being has got this incredible power that enables us to every possible achievement, if only we set our minds to it and develop tremendous focus on realizing our creative will.

THE MEMORY SURFACE

How our Memory Surface Works and Why Memory is Not Creative

In his book *Serious Creativity (1996)* Edward de Bono states that education does very little indeed about teaching creative thinking.

Over more than twenty years, de Bono stressed, he saw an astounding lack of creativity not only in schools, but also in business, and even in the highest ranks of government.

Edward de Bono's creativity model does not deal with artistic creativity, but with general creativity, and de Bono says that creativity can be learned, as it is but a special thinking skill or a mode of highly effective and holistic thinking which involves a technique that he called 'lateral thinking.'

Lateral thinking is not a special skill only of the right brain hemisphere, as de Bono pointed out in various publications, but a particularly coordinated way of both brain hemispheres working in harmony—in sync.

—See Edward de Bono, The Use of Lateral Thinking (1967).

The discovery of lateral thinking came about through de Bono's observation of the human brain's unique capability to collect and store information by pattern recognition and pattern assembly. This means in clear text that the brain does not store isolated pieces of information but always organizes information in patterns. De Bono states:

> What computers find so hard to do
> (pattern recognition) the brain does
> instantly and automatically.
>
> —Edward de Bono, Serious Creativity, 11.

When de Bono released his theory of passively organizing systems in one of his first books, *The Mechanism of Mind (1969)*, scientists at first disregarded his astonishing and genial findings. Later Nobel prize winners reconfirmed it, and the amazing new discoveries in neurology corroborate it brilliantly.

The preferred-pathways system of the brain, nowadays presented as common knowledge even in popular science books, is but another way of formulating de Bono's early theory. And de Bono equally saw the negative side of this system whereas neurologists continue to recognize but the positive effects of it. The essential negative point in passively organizing systems is that the recognition itself is conditioned upon the already existing patterns. Bono said that when we analyze data we can only pick out the idea we already have. And even more clearly:

> Most executives, many scientists, and almost all business school graduates believe that if you analyze data, this will give you new ideas.
> Unfortunately, this belief is totally wrong. The mind can only see what it is prepared to see.
>
> —Edward de Bono, Serious Creativity, 24.

That de Bono's insight is more than neurology is shown by the fact that no lesser than Krishnamurti equally taught that only passive awareness and not active thought can help to really understand the world intelligently.

Thought or what we call our ratio is not able to recognize patterns, it can only process patterns that are already stored away in the memory surface.

In addition, the conditioning of perception by thought and by past experience was one of the major arguments Krishnamurti used in order to overcome the limitations of the thought process and to show that there is unlimited intelligence and awareness not in thought but in the realm beyond thought.

To limit Edward de Bono's teachings to mere corporate training or thinking training would do injustice to this truly leading philosopher and perception trainer. Nowadays, holistic thinking experts take all this for granted, as it has happened with the revolutionary findings of Wilhelm Reich. At his life-time, he was rejected, while today he is silently copied. It is very similar with de Bono whose merits as a creative thinking pioneer cannot be underestimated.

Creativity, then, is not a product of thinking, strictly speaking, but of creative thinking which is more than thinking.

De Bono is very outspoken about the destructive process of creative thinking. What he calls the creative challenge basically consists in destroying existing patterns or just disregarding them in order to be able to free one's perception from their conditioning influence.

In this sense, creativity comes close to love, or love could be called a form of creativity. Interestingly, Krishnamurti stated that love is destructive in the sense that it destroys existing perception patterns and thus powerfully refreshes our regard on life, and on ourselves.

The same happens in moments when we are truly creative. It also happens, as de Bono repeatedly pointed out, in humor. Perhaps that is the reason why humor heals and exerts such a positive influence not only on our mind but also on our body and whole organism. The reason is that it detoxifies the body from accumulated old patterns that have restricted our evolution.

To understand this reasoning we should keep in mind that evolution can only take place where our regard shifts.

Evolution proceeds in a spiraled manner, repeating the basic processes of one level of evolution on the next while climbing one step higher on the evolutionary scale. The form of the DNS, symbol of all life, reminds it plastically. Our regard can only shift in moments where conditioning ends. This can happen during meditation or during what de Bono called 'the creative pause.'

Meditation in its original meaning is not what most people think it was. It's not sitting cross-legged and staring in the air. It is first of all silence, inward silence, and a slow-down of the rational thought processes, so as to give way to a heightened and acute, yet passive, awareness; passive in the sense of detachment but not passive in the sense of sluggishness or half-heartedness. There is to be lots of energy if acute awareness is to take place.

Edward de Bono did not talk about meditation. In his writings he hardly if ever made allusions to Eastern wisdom. However, it is possible to extract the wisdom that de Bono has developed and compare it with ancient Oriental wisdom.

The way de Bono develops creativity is based on what I would call 'active thinking,' a way of using thought that is not merely rational but that involves our right-brain capacities so as to bring about more holistic thought patterns.

It is quite different from the Eastern approach which can be said to rather start from the premise that we have to first stop thought in order to connect to the higher realm of wisdom and creative thinking. For de Bono, it is not to stop thinking but to think differently.

Another difference would be one of dynamics. Both approaches, the ancient Eastern approach to direct perception, and de Bono's, have in common that they stress the ultimate importance of the holistic perception process as such.

Again we can see that Krishnamurti's approach, although in many ways original and breaking with the tradition, was in this point confirming the oldest of traditions.

The perhaps most important part of K's spiritual teachings deals with perception, with how we use it, how we focus attention and how we can cope with conditioning that is inherent in every kind of perception.

However, in terms of the dynamics involved in the process of perception, the Western and the Eastern approaches differ. The Eastern approach starts from the premise that only by slowing down thought, by detaching from the thought content and by becoming passively aware, we open our perceptional antennas for new input and thus become creative.

The Western approach, as de Bono has developed it is in the contrary a very active and deliberate process of thinking to be learned and carried out that will trigger the creativity response. This difference in approaching the question typically represents the way Westerners and Orientals tend to think or to behave. It also makes clear what the essential difference is between creativity and creativeness.

De Bono's lateral thinking method is intentionally limited to business, not artistic creativity as a deliberate and effective way of thinking that delivers creative results on demand. It is not meant to be a way created for artists or people who live their lives in a way to constantly create—it is not meant to teach creativeness.

On the other hand, Krishnamurti's educational approach, as it flew out from his teaching and became the basis of the Krishnamurti schools in India, England and the United States definitely is a way to educate children for creativeness in an encompassing and spiritual sense.

—See J. Krishnamurti, Education and the Significance of Life, London: Victor Gollancz, 1978, J. Krishnamurti,

The Penguin Krishnamurti Reader, Part II: For the Young, London, New York: Penguin Books, 1987 and J. Krishnamurti, Beginnings of Learning, London, New York: Penguin Books, 1986.

PERCEPTION AND SPIRITUALITY

Why Perception is a Prime Topic in True Liberal

Spirituality

To repeat it, Edward de Bono's approach to enhancing creativity is based upon deliberate methods of lateral or holistic thinking in order to achieve practical results and to solve problems. It is not so much a lifestyle as in the case of Krishnamurti's teachings and can, on demand, be reproduced by any kind of individual whatever his or her general orientation may be.

De Bono has developed a rather pragmatic and sophisticated approach that requires repeated practice yet promises to produce results for everyone who seriously subscribes to it.

The systematic and rational way of teaching that is beyond mere ratio is very much akin to the Western mind, and particularly the mindset of Western managers. This fact explains in part the tremendous success that de Bono's teachings had even in Asia, where today, except perhaps Japan, it is the Western management style that is predominantly practiced in the corporate world.

I have used Edward de Bono's 'Six Hats Game' regularly in my seminars with corporations in Asia and was always successful with it. Successful in the sense that people had fun with it. Successful however not in the sense that they really could play the game. I would rather say that for most of my seminar participants, it was almost impossible to develop any creative ideas. In fact, associative or right-brain thinking has been almost invalidated by the school system and the utter disrespect of children's natural personal power and creativity that is the general attitude of teachers in most Asian countries. This is, by the way, something de Bono explicitly deplored in most of his books.

There is perhaps a general principle to observe, a principle that is often overlooked: we just cannot be effective if we do not embed all we do into the reigning culture.

When I say reigning culture I do not mean mainstream culture. We still may do our things and may have our niche in the long run, and we can very well live without the approval of the majority. But lacking out on the approval of the majority does not mean lacking out on integrating one's message into culture. Because culture means diversity. Culture means a range of opposites that are united under one and the same roof. Culture means a certain form of protection and it means a certain basic form of tolerance. Culture means curiosity and a sustainable form of artistic madness.

Let's look at a modern institution such as the Esalen Institute in Big Sur, California. It's really uncanny to see that it was not only artists and coaches, but also top managers of large multinationals who in the United States introduced the perennial techniques such as direct perception into the postmodern business culture. It was not scholars, and it was certainly not priests, despite the fact that while direct perception was not part of the official Church philosophy, the ones who possessed this knowledge in the past were scholars and saints. Now enlightenment also comes from top managers—which is an interesting new development in the New Age culture.

In the past, as I mentioned before, perception was taught as a part of high-level spiritual teaching. This was certainly so in theosophy, but theosophy was in this point inspired by the oldest of spiritual traditions in India, as reflected in the Vedas.

Typically, qualified gurus in India, when you talk to them, come very quickly to talk about perception and the pitfalls of perception, and for good reason. Without clear perception and a deliberate purification of the many projections that the untrained mind is suffering from, we cannot get an adequate picture of reality. What we get is smoke, said Krishnamurti. I would say we get a distorted picture of reality and in addition take this distorted picture, because of our natural observer bias as the reality. And this without seeing the relativity of our personal reality and the fact that all reality perceived by a human being is personal reality.

Many mediums today transmit messages of similar content. The richest to be found here is perhaps what Jane Roberts transcribed from the SETH spirit in her books *The Nature of Personal Reality (1994)* and *The Nature of the Psyche (1996)*.

> —See also Wendy Munro: Journey into a New Millennium (Transmissions from Sirius): A Cosmic Account of the Millennial Transformation for Humanity and Planet Earth (1997) and Barbara Marciniak, Bringers of the Dawn: Teachings from the Pleiadians (1992).

Today, the importance of perception, and consciousness about the observer bias form more and more part of an expanded and holistic science paradigm.

The paradigm shift in consciousness research has come about mainly through quantum physics, which shows that the observer is always entangled in the process of observation and cannot, as Newtonian science believed, be isolated from it. This has been made very clear also in a recent popular film entitled *What the Bleep Do We Know (2005/2006)*.

> —William Arntz, William & Betsy Chasse, What the Bleep Do We Know, 20th Century Fox, 2005 (DVD), Down The Rabbit Hole Quantum Edition, 20th Century Fox, 2006 (3 DVD Set).

When we begin to understand that on the level of consciousness, which also has been called the quantum level, all is connected, we cannot seriously continue to give our children a highly fragmented education, but we have to take the learning of geniuses and genius children as examples of how to structure new learning curricula.

It will then become obvious that we have to form links between all matters to be learnt by associative networks rather than presenting the learning stuff in a linear and logical, or hierarchical manner.

This will naturally imply and strengthen the right brain hemisphere in children that in traditional education is badly neglected if not outright shunned by the obsessional focus upon left-brain deductive logic and isolated topic-based memorization.

Memorization, then, that is in accordance with the natural learning capabilities of our brain, will be based on a better understanding of preferred pathways, neuronal connections and their intelligence, the insight in the non-hierarchical nature of life and all knowledge about life, a systems view of life and last not least, the ultimate insight that all true intelligence is patterned intelligence.

BIBLIOGRAPHY

Contextual Bibliography

ARIÈS, PHILIPPE

Centuries of Childhood
NEW YORK: VINTAGE BOOKS, 1962

ARNTZ, WILLIAM & CHASSE, BETSY

What the Bleep Do We Know
20TH CENTURY FOX, 2005 (DVD)

Down The Rabbit Hole Quantum Edition
20TH CENTURY FOX, 2006 (3 DVD SET)

COVITZ, JOEL

Emotional Child Abuse
THE FAMILY CURSE
BOSTON: SIGO PRESS, 1986

DeMause, Lloyd

The History of Childhood
New York, 1974

Foundations of Psychohistory
New York: Creative Roots, 1982

Diamond, Stephen A., May, Rollo

Anger, Madness, and the Daimonic
The Psychological Genesis of Violence, Evil and Creativity
New York: State University of New York Press, 1999

DiCarlo, Russell E. (Ed.)

Towards A New World View
Conversations at the Leading Edge
Erie, PA: Epic Publishing, 1996

Eisler, Riane

The Chalice and the Blade
Our history, Our future
San Francisco: Harper & Row, 1995

Sacred Pleasure: Sex, Myth and the Politics of the Body
New Paths to Power and Love
San Francisco: Harper & Row, 1996

The Partnership Way
New Tools for Living and Learning
With David Loye
Brandon, VT: Holistic Education Press, 1998

CONTEXTUAL BIBLIOGRAPHY

The Real Wealth of Nations
CREATING A CARING ECONOMICS
SAN FRANCISCO: BERRETT-KOEHLER PUBLISHERS, 2008

ELLIS, HAVELOCK

Sexual Inversion
REPUBLISHED
NEW YORK: UNIVERSITY PRESS OF THE PACIFIC, 2001
ORIGINALLY PUBLISHED IN 1897

The Sexual Impulse in Women
REPUBLISHED
NEW YORK: UNIVERSITY PRESS OF THE PACIFIC, 2001
ORIGINALLY PUBLISHED IN 1903

The Dance of Life
NEW YORK: GREENWOOD PRESS REPRINT EDITION, 1973
ORIGINALLY PUBLISHED IN 1923

ERICKSON, MILTON H.

My Voice Will Go With You
THE TEACHING TALES OF MILTON H. ERICKSON
BY SIDNEY ROSEN (ED.)
NEW YORK: NORTON & CO., 1991

Complete Works 1.0, CD-ROM
NEW YORK: MILTON H. ERICKSON FOUNDATION, 2001

FREUD, SIGMUND

The Interpretation of Dreams
NEW YORK: AVON, REISSUE EDITION, 1980

AND IN: THE STANDARD EDITION OF THE COMPLETE PSYCHOLOGICAL
WORKS OF SIGMUND FREUD , (24 VOLUMES) ED. BY JAMES STRACHEY
NEW YORK: W. W. NORTON & COMPANY, 1976

Totem and Taboo
NEW YORK: ROUTLEDGE, 1999
ORIGINALLY PUBLISHED IN 1913

FROMM, ERICH

The Anatomy of Human Destructiveness
NEW YORK: OWL BOOK, 1992
ORIGINALLY PUBLISHED IN 1973

Escape from Freedom
NEW YORK: OWL BOOKS, 1994
ORIGINALLY PUBLISHED IN 1941
TO HAVE OR TO BE
NEW YORK: CONTINUUM INTERNATIONAL PUBLISHING, 1996
ORIGINALLY PUBLISHED IN 1976

The Art of Loving
NEW YORK: HARPERPERENNIAL, 2000
ORIGINALLY PUBLISHED IN 1956

GOLEMAN, DANIEL

Emotional Intelligence
NEW YORK, BANTAM BOOKS, 1995

HAMEROFF, NEWBERG, WOOLF, BIERMAN

Consciousness
20 SCIENTISTS INTERVIEWED
DIRECTOR: GREGORY ALSBURY

CONTEXTUAL BIBLIOGRAPHY

5 DVD BOX SET, 540 MIN.
NEW YORK: ALSBURY FILMS, 2003

JAMES, WILLIAM

Writings 1902-1910
THE VARIETIES OF RELIGIOUS EXPERIENCE / PRAGMATISM / A PLURALISTIC
UNIVERSE / THE MEANING OF TRUTH / SOME PROBLEMS OF PHILOSOPHY /
ESSAYS
NEW YORK: LIBRARY OF AMERICA, 1988

JUNG, CARL GUSTAV

Archetypes of the Collective Unconscious
IN: THE BASIC WRITINGS OF C.G. JUNG
NEW YORK: THE MODERN LIBRARY, 1959, 358-407

Collected Works
NEW YORK, 1959

On the Nature of the Psyche
IN: THE BASIC WRITINGS OF C.G. JUNG
NEW YORK: THE MODERN LIBRARY, 1959, 47-133

Psychological Types
COLLECTED WRITINGS, VOL. 6
PRINCETON: PRINCETON UNIVERSITY PRESS, 1971

Psychology and Religion
IN: THE BASIC WRITINGS OF C.G. JUNG
NEW YORK: THE MODERN LIBRARY, 1959, 582-655

Religious and Psychological Problems of Alchemy
IN: THE BASIC WRITINGS OF C.G. JUNG
NEW YORK: THE MODERN LIBRARY, 1959, 537-581

PATTERNS OF PERCEPTION

The Basic Writings of C.G. Jung
NEW YORK: THE MODERN LIBRARY, 1959

The Development of Personality
COLLECTED WRITINGS, VOL. 17
PRINCETON: PRINCETON UNIVERSITY PRESS, 1954

The Meaning and Significance of Dreams
BOSTON: SIGO PRESS, 1991

The Myth of the Divine Child
IN: ESSAYS ON A SCIENCE OF MYTHOLOGY
PRINCETON, N.J.: PRINCETON UNIVERSITY PRESS BOLLINGEN
SERIES XXII, 1969. (WITH KARL KERENYI)

Two Essays on Analytical Psychology
COLLECTED WRITINGS, VOL. 7
PRINCETON: PRINCETON UNIVERSITY PRESS, 1972
FIRST PUBLISHED BY ROUTLEDGE & KEGAN PAUL, LTD., 1953

KOESTLER, ARTHUR

The Act of Creation
NEW YORK: PENGUIN ARKANA, 1989.
ORIGINALLY PUBLISHED IN 1964

KRISHNAMURTI, J.

Freedom From The Known
SAN FRANCISCO: HARPER & ROW, 1969

The First and Last Freedom
SAN FRANCISCO: HARPER & ROW, 1975

Education and the Significance of Life
LONDON: VICTOR GOLLANCZ, 1978

CONTEXTUAL BIBLIOGRAPHY

Commentaries on Living
FIRST SERIES
LONDON: VICTOR GOLLANCZ, 1985

Commentaries on Living
SECOND SERIES
LONDON: VICTOR GOLLANCZ, 1986

Krishnamurti's Journal
LONDON: VICTOR GOLLANCZ, 1987

Krishnamurti's Notebook
LONDON: VICTOR GOLLANCZ, 1986

Beyond Violence
LONDON: VICTOR GOLLANCZ, 1985

Beginnings of Learning
NEW YORK: PENGUIN, 1986

The Penguin Krishnamurti Reader
NEW YORK: PENGUIN, 1987

On God
SAN FRANCISCO: HARPER & ROW, 1992

On Fear
SAN FRANCISCO: HARPER & ROW, 1995

The Essential Krishnamurti
SAN FRANCISCO: HARPER & ROW, 1996

The Ending of Time
WITH DR. DAVID BOHM
SAN FRANCISCO: HARPER & ROW, 1985

LIEDLOFF, JEAN

Continuum Concept
IN SEARCH OF HAPPINESS LOST
NEW YORK: PERSEUS BOOKS, 1986
FIRST PUBLISHED IN 1977

MOORE, THOMAS

Care of the Soul
A GUIDE FOR CULTIVATING DEPTH AND SACREDNESS IN EVERYDAY LIFE
NEW YORK: HARPER & COLLINS, 1994

ROSEN, SYDNEY (ED.)

My Voice Will Go With You
THE TEACHING TALES OF MILTON H. ERICKSON
NEW YORK: NORTON & CO., 1991STEIN, ROBERT M.

Redeeming the Inner Child in Marriage and Therapy
IN: RECLAIMING THE INNER CHILD
ED. BY JEREMIAH ABRAMS
NEW YORK: TARCHER/PUTNAM, 1990, 261 FF.

STEINER, RUDOLF

Theosophy
AN INTRODUCTION TO THE SPIRITUAL PROCESSES IN HUMAN LIFE
AND IN THE COSMOS
NEW YORK: ANTHROPOSOPHIC PRESS, 1994

CONTEXTUAL BIBLIOGRAPHY

STONE, HAL & STONE, SIDRA

Embracing Our Selves
THE VOICE DIALOGUE MANUAL
SAN RAFAEL, CA: NEW WORLD LIBRARY, 1989

SZASZ, THOMAS

The Myth of Mental Illness
NEW YORK: HARPER & ROW, 1984

TART, CHARLES T.

Altered States of Consciousness
A BOOK OF READINGS
HOBOKEN, N.J.: WILEY & SONS, 1969

WHAT THE BLEEP DO WE KNOW!?

See Arntz, William

WHITFIELD, CHARLES L.

Healing the Child Within
DEERFIELD BEACH, FL: HEALTH COMMUNICATIONS, 1987

Personal Notes